THE GIFT
OF COLOURING

FOR
MUM

Michael O'Mara Books Limited

First published in Great Britain in 2016 by
Michael O'Mara Books Limited
9 Lion Yard
Tremadoc Road
London SW4 7NQ

A CIP catalogue record for this book is available from the British Library.

Papers used by Michael O'Mara Books Limited are natural, recyclable products made from wood grown in sustainable forests. The manufacturing processes conform to the environmental regulations of the country of origin.

ISBN: 978-1-78243-583-9

1 2 3 4 5 6 7 8 9 10

www.mombooks.com

Cover design by Ana Bjezancevic

Illustrations by Sam Loman, Jo Taylor, Louise Wright, Julie Ingham, Michelle Breen, Jake McDonald, Pimlada Phuapradit, Lizzie Preston, Emily Hamilton

Cover illustration by Cindy Wilde

Printed and bound in China

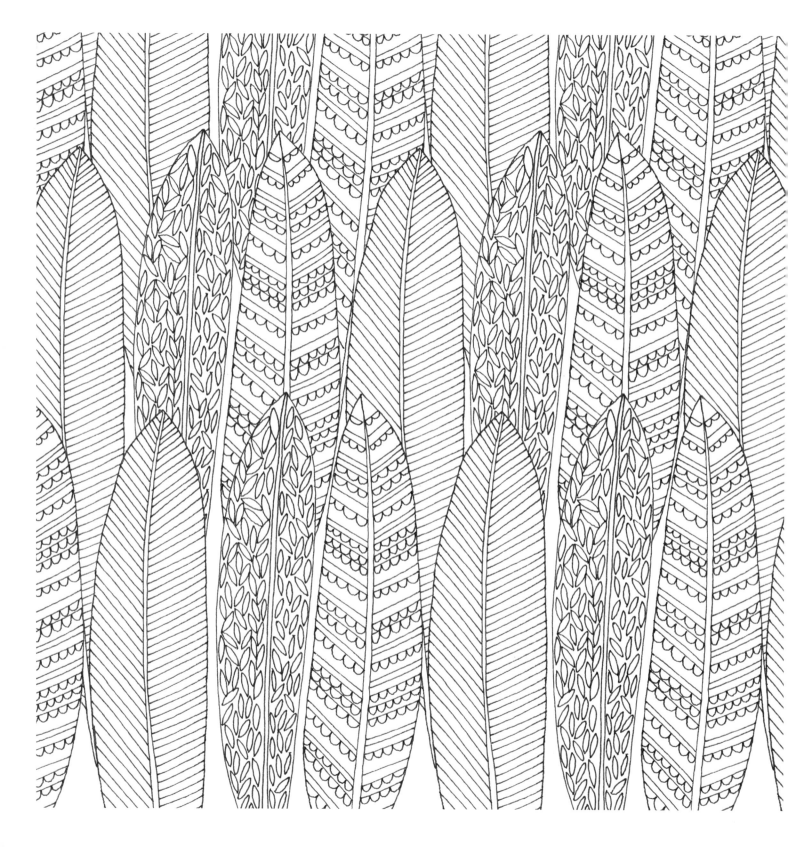

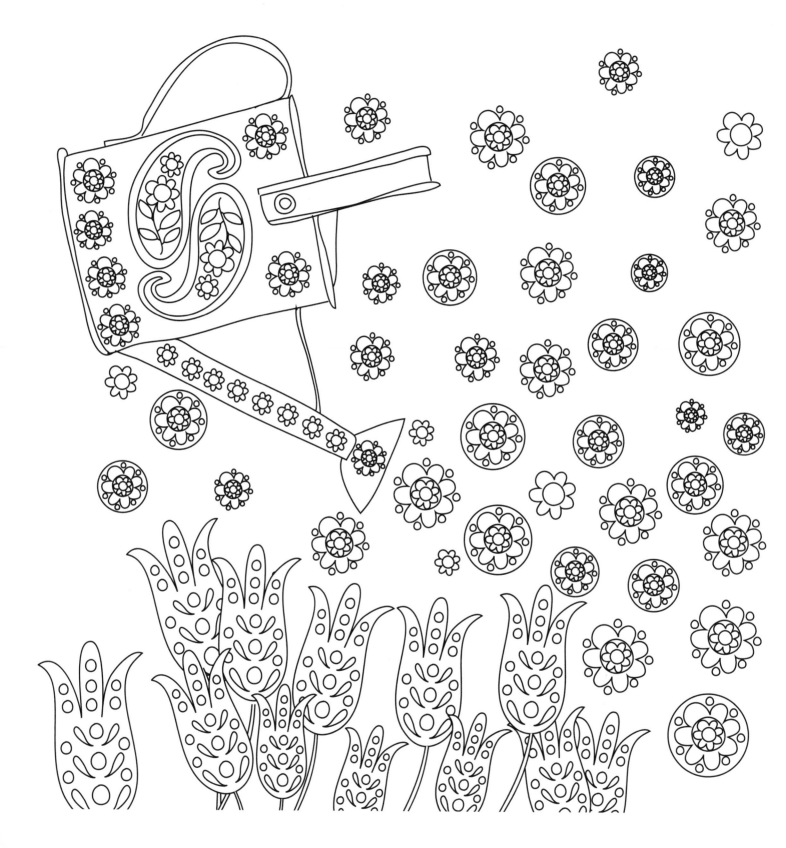

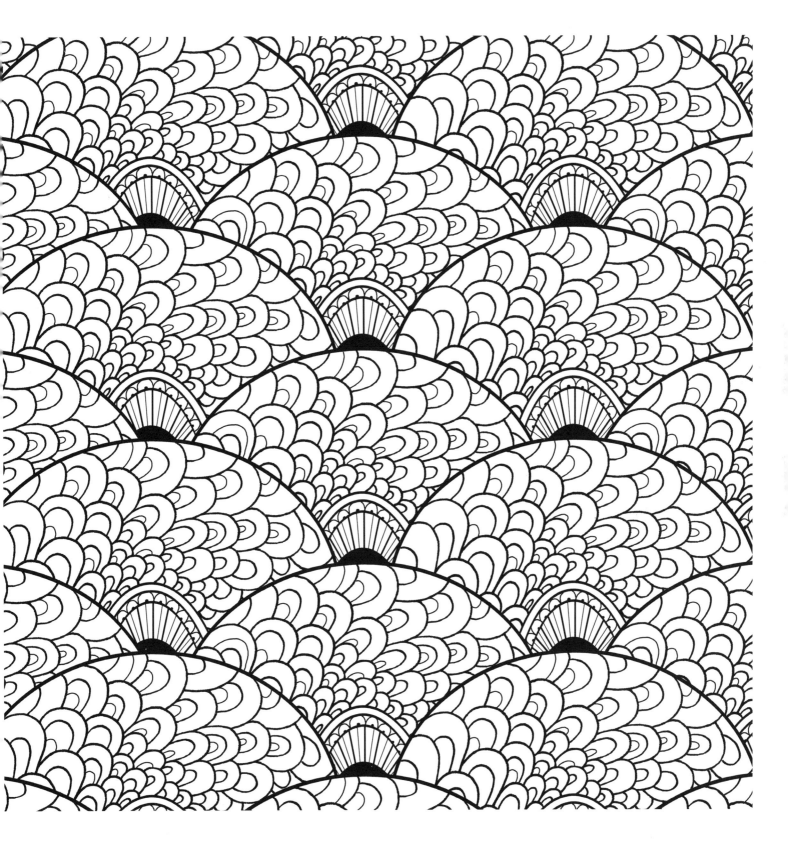

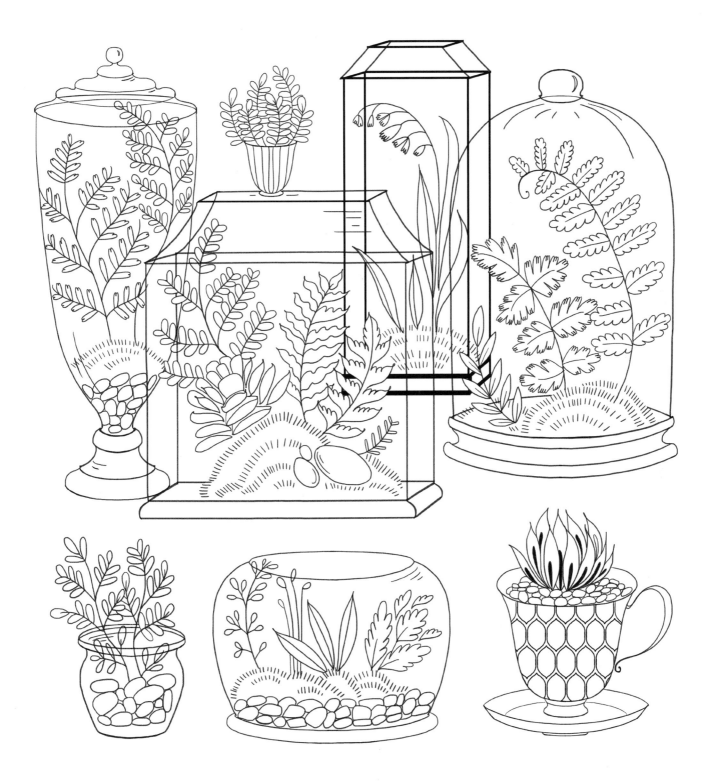

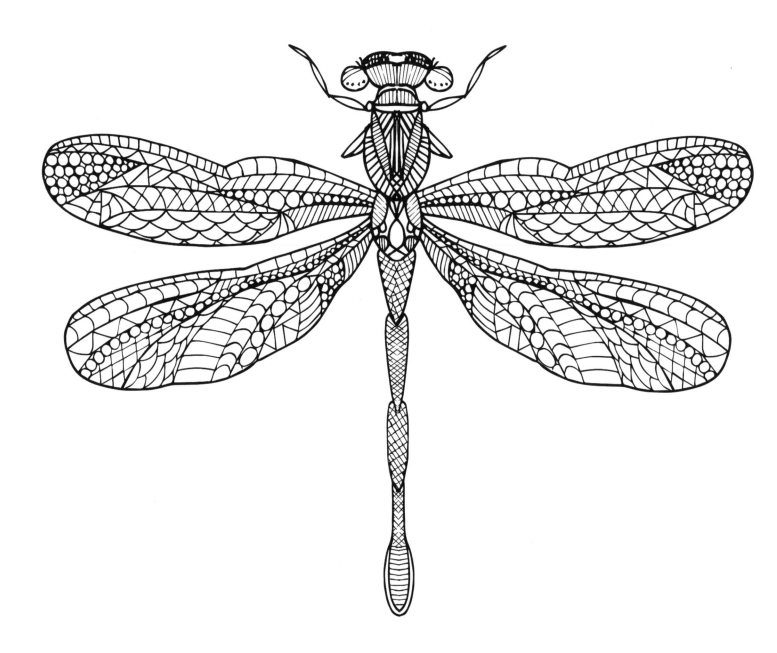

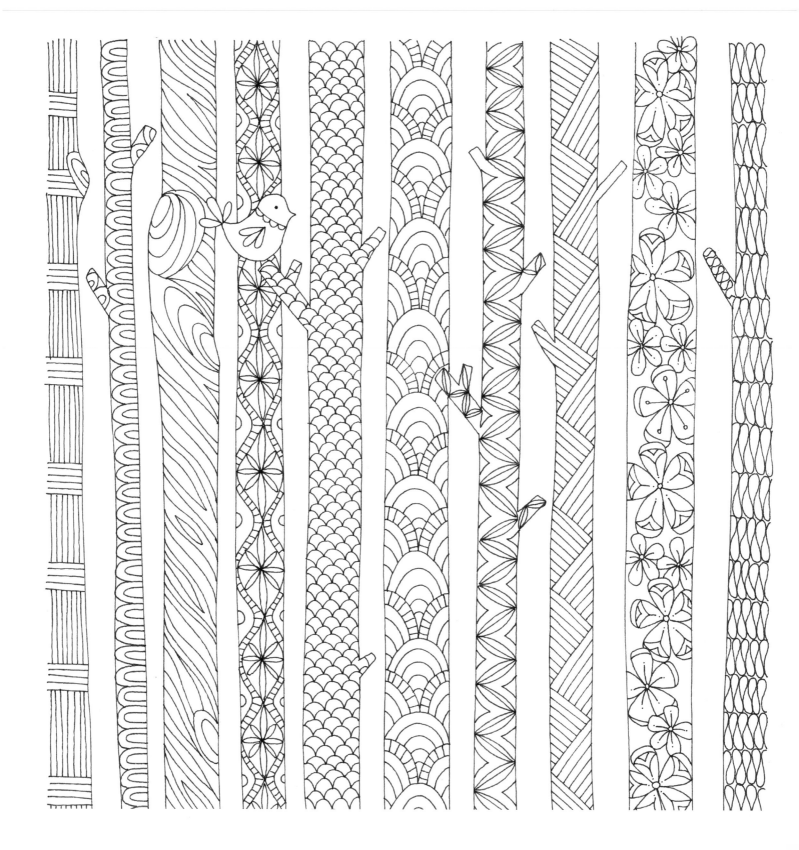

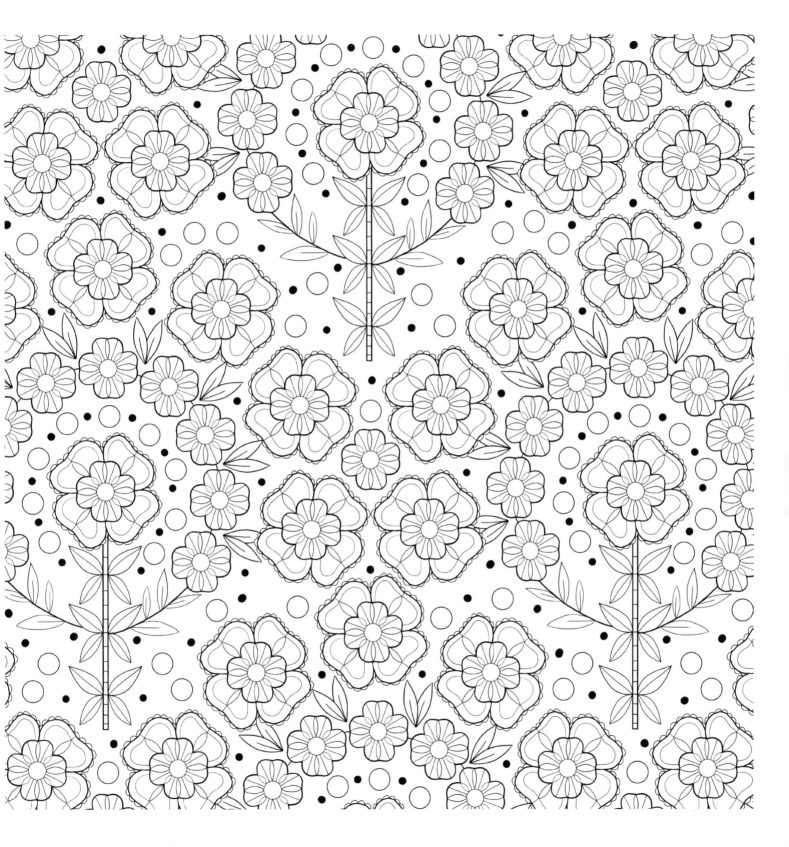

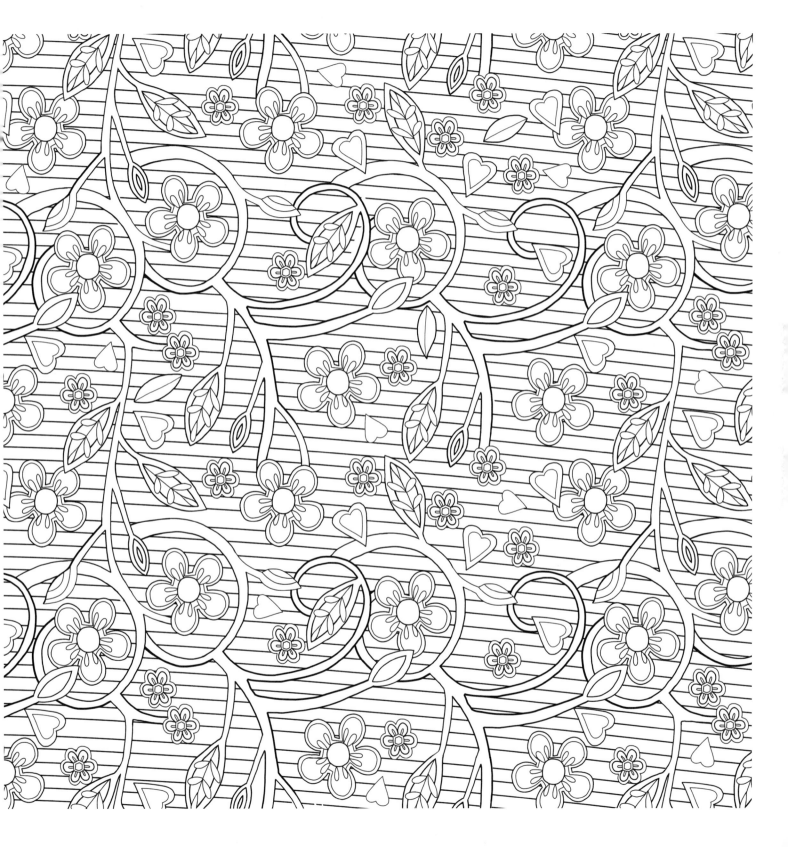

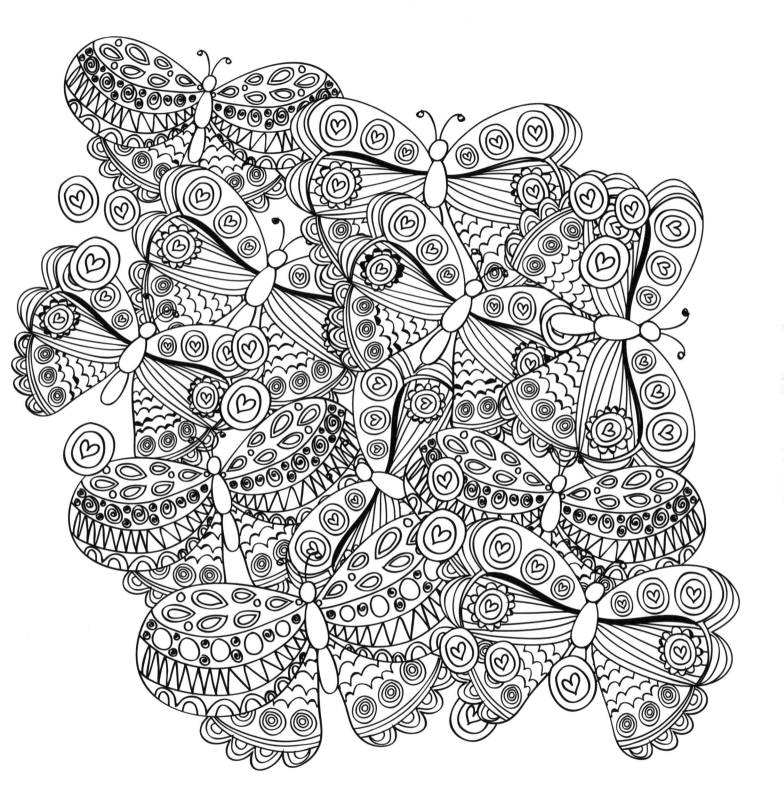

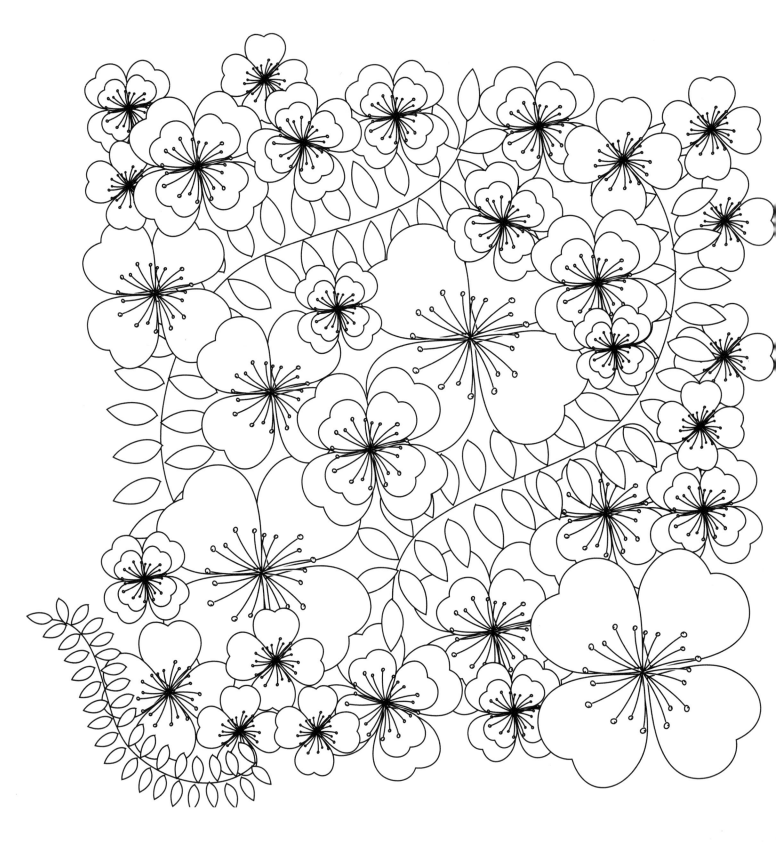